CROSSING CULTURES

CROSSING CULTURES

THE AFRICAN WORLDVIEW AMIDST
CONTEMPORARY CULTURES

Trophimus Odie

XULON PRESS

Xulon Press
2301 Lucien Way #415
Maitland, FL 32751
407.339.4217
www.xulonpress.com

xulon PRESS

Printed in the United States of America.

ISBN-13: 978-1-6305-05585

DEDICATION

To my beloved wife, Lena Odie, who has been my biggest inspiration and a motivator for the writing of this book. I remember the first time you encouraged me to write a book was at the resort during our honeymoon. I must say, eight years is a long time to wait, but here is the fulfillment of your encouragement.

To my children, Gabriel Odie, Hannah Odie, and Malachi Odie – you are neither strangers nor visitors to these cultures, but rather descendants of the fact, a sign and a testimony of what God does with hearts that are willing. May you teach these values to your children so that they will, in like manner, teach their children.

TABLE OF CONTENTS

ACKNOWLEDGMENTS

I am thankful for the contributions and insights that various people have made to this book. I am particularly grateful to Danielle Weber, for her tireless work in typing the first draft from our numerous conversations. I must thank Joseph Ssemutooke, for the extensive research work for the book. A huge thanks to Richard Otto and Isaac Kaweesa for verifying that the writings are a true representation of the cultures, and finally, my sincere thanks to the team at Xulon Press for making this dream a reality.

Key thoughts to take note of before delving into this work:

Generalizations about the culture of the continent and many other aspects of African life are not easy to make because it is not one homogeneous cultural area. The continent is marked by great cultural and linguistic diversities, primarily the differences are along country and ethnic lines. A statement that can be made about one country or ethnic group may be altogether inapplicable to another, even in the same geographical sub-region. Therefore, it is imperative for readers to understand the work done in trying to aggregate the variety of cultural aspects of the different African communities, by identifying common denominators and building around them. A hard job but, hopefully, one fairly well accomplished here.

BACKGROUND

A t some point in your life, you have probably heard the African proverb, "It takes a village to raise a child." Certainly, this is true. But I also believe that when that child is grown, he takes the village with him. At least, this was the case for me.

The following is an attempt to share examples of our culture, which I believe non-Africans coming into contact with Africans will find especially handy and will be grateful they are armed with. I've seen and experienced a great deal, but one of the things that have compelled me to share these thoughts with you is what I have witnessed in people's reception of one another. This is true for me, when moving to North America, as well as the Africans' reception of foreigners. Thus, I believe that this book will be helpful for any native of the Western hemisphere traveling to Africa as a missionary, tourist, or prospective settler.

Both for Africans as well as Westerners, there is an unintentional disconnect that exists because the culture is simply different from what non-Africans know. At the outset, this may seem irreparable, but it always helps to remember that any two cultures have differences, no matter how geographically close they may be. Proximity has little to do with the fact that linguistics, society, and history all play a role in the adaptation of the people living in a particular location. When we take this into account, it is easier to adapt the mantra that *different* is not synonymous with *wrong*. I am not implying that this cannot be the case, but it should never be our intention to meet someone and coerce them into our way of life just because we are not familiar with theirs.

One issue widely discussed in our society today is the acceptance of others. Even if we aren't familiar with their ways, or don't hold the same beliefs, it is vital that we show them the respect and love which they naturally deserve as human beings. This same mindset also applies to people who are going to live in other countries.

I can share from experience that adjusting to another culture is challenging, but I would like this book to also alter the perspective of those few who come to Africa with the intention of trying to change everything.

I have learned that there is a significant difference between cultures, and while that may be an obvious statement, the profound realization is that none of them are necessarily wrong. The entire history of mankind is engulfed in the belief that our own ways are correct, and that people of other cultures need to learn and adapt to our ways. Examples of this can be seen throughout time and throughout the world. Common instances are: Romans trying to conquer Greece, Spain trying to conquer the Aztec Empire, and even the Norman conquest of England.

What was the collective purpose of this? Well, land acquisition, of course. And granted, this was usually sorted out by war, but what was the final result? The country that won always went about changing the ways of the conquered people. In essence, the majority changed the minority, and the original cultural values were all but lost.

Certainly, we are talking about a different scale and proportions here, but I think that the general idea is the same. While it won't always be done forcefully or with violence, it is a fact that no matter where you go in this world, people will always try to change others based on what their view of *right* is. It's not necessarily even intentional, but we are simply more comfortable with the known than the unknown. Yet, as the person who is the unknown one in the situation, it feels both uncomfortable to be unknown, as well as uncomfortable to be made to change, so we need to remember to let people adapt in their own time.

My sincere hope is that this book will be of great help to you on your exciting adventure into Africa, whether as a visitor (tourist, short-term missions, business traveler, student, or researcher), or if you are adventuring into the continent for a considerably long period (marrying into it, moving as an expatriate or as a missionary). The things you will see will undoubtedly surprise you, and there may be times when *culture shock* is all too real of a term, however all human beings thrive on love and so, let the take-away message be to treat others as you would want to be treated.

Introductory Notes About Africa

Away from the continent, Africa is commonly regarded as a single large country to be lined up alongside the likes of France, Brazil, and Germany. But nothing could be further from the truth. For Africa is not just one of earth's seven continents, but one of the largest, most diverse, and most complex continents. With fifty-four independent nations accounting for one-fifth of the earth's entire land surface, Africa has a history that arguably predates that of every other continent, a population that can be divided into more than one-thousand ethnic divisions, the world's largest desert, as well as the world's most favorable conditions for agriculture, and clusters of some of the world's richest people interspersed among some of the world's poorest people. The continent of Africa truly contains a diversity of cultures and beliefs.

It is, therefore, for the purpose of having you delve into this book with a proper impression of Africa, that the following overview of Africa has been provided. It is also important to note that the details provided below focus a great deal on Sub-Saharan Africa, otherwise referred to as "Black Africa" or "Africa Proper." That is, the part of Africa that lies south of the Sahara Desert and is primarily inhabited by dark-skinned people – this excludes the Arabs, who primarily inhabit the continent's northern portion engulfing the Sahara Desert and who are not necessarily dark-skinned. Here, it might be noted, too, that besides not being dark, the Arabs inhabiting the northern part of the continent also distinctly differ from the rest of Africa in culture, lifestyle, and history, among other aspects in which Sub-Saharan Africa might be said to have a bold common denominator.

1 - PERCEPTION

"The best source of information about the forest is always from the monkey." — African proverb.

As a little boy discovering the world around me, far back in the day, I heard stories about tribes who allegedly ate human flesh. This affected the way I interacted with people from those tribes. I tried to avoid getting close to them and always watched my back when in their presence, lest I got too close to people who ate human flesh and learned their evil culinary practice, or became their meal. For example, at school or church, I avoided sitting or playing with boys from such tribes. So much that even when I needed something from someone from that tribe, I'd rather do without it than ask them, and I would never accept any help from them when they offered it. (Please note: In Africa, and particularly in Uganda, there are so many tribes and ethnic groups that are greatly feared).

The fearsome stories told about other tribes (such as eating human flesh or practicing witchcraft) were mostly born of biases and prejudices. Biases and prejudices born of mere failure to understand or appreciate a different culture, others were born of utter malice and some of a combination of these issues. For example, if people from one tribe were inventing stories to warn their children about wandering about the neighborhood, they painted some neighboring tribes in a bad light – tribes with whom they happened to have a rivalry or tribes whose lifestyle they despised.

It wasn't until I went to school and interacted with people from the so-called *bad tribes* that I eventually became enlightened. Off came the veil of ignorance which had created, in my mind, biases, and prejudices about these tribes.

The kind of bias and prejudice I have illustrated above is one of the big problems one has to face when moving into another culture and adjusting to their values, practices, and traditions. It can bring about bigger problems if you leave Africa and assimilate into Western society.

Over my time living in Canada, I have noticed that some people in North America have a preconceived notion of what Africa is like. They may use their perception of the continent, as a whole, to fit you into that preconceived idea of African people. Unfortunately, that preconceived notion/perception is usually an inaccurate and uneducated one. It doesn't take long to realize that some people think of Africa as a hellish place where nothing good exists and from which nothing good can come. You may notice that people think of Africa as a continent rife with war, disease, hunger, and extreme forms of poverty and deprivation, which won't help you acculturate when you have come from there.

Misinterpretations Originating from the Media

The perception illustrated above is primarily a result of media reporting. It seems that no matter the media, they never paint Africa as a place that holds any goodness or where people have anything productive, progressive, or successful. The communications industry has created a floating world, the intent or purpose of which is difficult to fathom. This media consistently and exclusively paints Africa in negative terms, showing only the terrible side of the continent and never the positive, or good side.

But this biased perception or preconceived notion of Africa is very far from reality. Unfortunately, it is only through traveling that an ordinary person from the West can discover the true side of Africa and understand what a skewed impression they have learned from the media.

The problems which are shown by the media do, indeed, exist across the continent, but they are not the end of the continent's narrative. Beyond disease, hunger, war, and all those other struggles which the media exclusively captures, Africa is a place where people exist – enjoying eating regular meals and living in peaceful societies that aren't constantly at war.

It's even more sobering for those who travel to African countries with existing biases/prejudices, and they find that the greatest percentage of people are healthy, multitudes have been educated, a good number of citizens are financially stable, and with some very wealthy.

Prejudice and Bias

While our misconceptions about other people may often be the product of ignorance and inaccuracies, most of the time, we don't admit to being ignorant and misinformed. A core misconception of many is thinking of Africa as a country rather than a continent. It is quite common to hear comments such as, "I plan to visit Africa in the spring," or "I just returned from Africa last June."

Statements such as these have made Africa look like one small, uniform country.

African's False Image of the Western World

The unenlightened perception isn't something held by only the Westerners and suffered by only Africans who move to the West. Africans also have a twisted perception of the Western world, and consequently Western people who find themselves in Africa also have to make do with biases and prejudices.

Africans look at people from developed economies as being superior and strong. They tend to think that everyone who lives in a Western country is rich, always has money and doesn't need to work. Here, it isn't so much a problem of mainstream media presenting incorrect information to Africa, more so it is a glorified image of the West that Hollywood has portrayed, which has made everyone from developed countries appear as wealthy in the eyes of most Africans.

One time a certain man told me that, since I had married a Caucasian, I was swimming in money. I told the man that it was to the contrary because I now had much higher expenses to work towards, more so than if I had married an African lady. I gave him the example that in order to go see my wife's parents, we, as a family unit, would need a significantly higher amount of funds to travel, yet if I had married a Ugandan, the highest cost I could ever possibly incur on public transport, even by traveling to the farthest place in the country, would be fifty Canadian dollars. Also, not to mention that you spend more on things like housing, transportation, and food because Caucasians are accustomed to a certain way of life. The things Africans consider a luxury are actually viewed as necessities in the West. Africans also typically view Caucasians as selfish. They have this impression that whenever Caucasians come to Africa, they look at their own selfish advantages. They do not understand that many people travel for business, development work, social networking, and missionary work. Rather, they tend to cluster most Westerners as people who have come for their own personal gains.

You might primarily blame this on the history of Western colonization in Africa, where Western people primarily moved there to rule the people and carry off its natural resources, including human capital that was carried off in the slave trade. This history still influences most Africans' views of Westerners, even to this day.

Africans also look at Western people as morally fallen and uncultured. This is largely a result of the movies they see. Scenes of near nudity, minimal clothing, freedom of sexual expressions, indiscriminate sexual relations, etc. They look at the movies and assume that what they see is the general lifestyle of Western people.

Africans' twisted perceptions of the Western world are partly because many people in the rural areas (who are the majority), lack the ability/means to know what is going on elsewhere. Many don't have access to Western media channels, and some are illiterate, or their world-view is parochial because they acquired only a very elementary education. Most impressions are from the movies which are cheaply available everywhere, and from hearsay from the elites, who themselves present a biased image.

The irony of this particular bias is that before the colonization of Africa by the Western world, a lot of nudity and minimal dressings were ingrained in the culture. Many years after colonization, there has been a paradigm shift in both parties. While the Western world leaned more and more towards liberalism and free-thinking, Africa became more conservative and traditional.

In this regard, many Africans who travel are shocked when what they see is far from their expectations. Those who travel expecting to obtain money easily, without hard work, are surprised that, in the West, money is hard-earned. They get even more shocked to see very poor (even homeless) people. Bias and prejudices go both ways, hence proper education and illumination of both cultures are definitely inconsequential.

Blessing in Diversity

"When a hyena wants to eat its children, it first
accuses them of smelling like goats"
— African proverb

Aside from perception, the reality is that some of the western nations boast of over 100 years of independence and self-rule, as opposed to many African countries with the majority gaining independence in the 1960s, with exceptions to Liberia, a colony of repatriated Africans formerly held in American slavery, attaining independence in 1847, the republic of South Africa in 1931 and, of course, not forgetting Ethiopia who are historically independent. With this in mind, an African moving or traveling to the western world for the very first time will seem like someone waking up from Dream. Everything is fast-paced and the traveler will need to accelerate his/her mind to come to speed with what is normal to Western people. When I moved to Canada, I was fortunate to travel at the beginning of spring, which gave me a glimpse of the cold weather, but still moderate enough for me to smoothly transition to summertime, then to fall, and the winter months, as expected.

The only thing I can compare winter season with that is understandable to an African is war. With the only difference being that war is sometimes unexpected, but you can always count on having a winter season every year. This season that takes up six months of the year, and up to eight months in some regions in different western countries, with temperatures dropping to as low as negative fifty degrees Centigrade in some areas, contributes greatly to the thought process and perception of the West. A lot has to be put into consideration when preparing for this expected catastrophe. Infrastructure, food supplies, appropriate clothing, road safety, and emergency response, just to mention a few. All these necessities need to be in place to enable people go through the winter months with ease. The three weapons, I should say, that the West has utilized very well to manage their affairs is, knowledge, time and speed. We won't go into details to break down these three things, but briefly, people concentrate on doing things they are familiar with and specialize in doing it. When it's time to sow seeds or harvest, the farmers will be doing that. And finally, they don't have the whole year to do some of these things, so they do them as fast and efficiently as possible because there is only a certain window of time in which people can work before temperatures start to change.

A philosophy held by many African people is captured in this Swahili proverb.

"POLE POLE NDIO MWENDO" and "HARAKA HARAKA HAINA BARAKA," which basically means that, "Slowness is the better locomotion" and "Hurry, hurry, has no blessings."

People strive at being steady and keen when performing given tasks and do not hurry for the sake of completing it. This can be explained by the fact that they are raised as free-range in the wild – hunting, farming, and living in simplicity. Some people enjoy life in that style, and don't even want to be bothered with sophisticated innovations and ideas. An example follows.

During colonial times, the British introduced cotton growing in Uganda amongst the Basogo tribe. This didn't go well, since the Basoga felt that they were forced to plant a lot of this foreign crop and at a breathtaking speed, and consequently, they watered the plants with hot water. A traveler, therefore, should prepare to slow down because people will generally slow you down if you don't. This kind of reluctance and lack of ambition may be seen by fast-paced people as probably derived from the fact the food grows at any given time of the year, and in most places in the continent. People won't have the same sense of urgency when it comes to TIME as it is in the west, the reason being that there isn't any expected drastic weather change like an oncoming winter. The weather will simply either be rainy or sunny.

Nonetheless, much as the systems in Western civilization were put in place with the sole purpose of making life comfortable for Western people, And the Africans set up their communities and ideologies, not having Westerners in mind. We now live in a global community interconnected in various ways and dependent on each other's economies and so we should strive to enjoy the blessings that diversity brings.

2 - IDENTITY

The child of a rat is a rat. – Malagasy Proverb

Identity

African people derive individual identity from communal identity. In simple terms, people address situations with words such as "ours" rather than "mine" and "we instead of "I", even if it was a one-man effort to accomplish something. An example is – if we, as a family, had previously expressed a desire to build a family house on our ancestral land, and at the moment I have the capacity to build, and go ahead and build the house, if I was asked about the project, I would then say "we" are building to include the rest of my siblings since they equally had the same idea but at the moment, I have the capacity. This is one of the ways generosity and selflessness have been cultivated in people's lives. It is a fact Africans traditionally never consciously identify themselves as independent of their communal identity. When that thought process does happen today, it is a learned behavior that has been adopted from the West and Asia. In African culture, it is primarily through relations with one's community and surroundings that an individual becomes a person of authority, whose actions and decisions affect the entire group rather than just oneself. These identities include clans, tribes, and groups, nations and countries, even the continent as a whole.

These identities start at the family level, then go upward to the clan level, tribal/ethnic level, national level, and even the continental level.

A typical Nigerian, for example, is primarily identified by their tribe as depicted by their name(s). So, before you get to know details about an individual, you already know his/her tribe. Tribal names are extremely common, as everyone has one or more. It is therefore not uncommon for two people to, immediately after meeting each other, begin to refer to one another as *brothers* or *sisters*, because upon saying your name, a person can already tell so much about your communal identity.

Almost every African culture follows the concept of "ubuntu," a term meaning "humanity." The word is often translated as "I am because we are," and also "humanity towards others," but is often used in a more philosophical sense to mean "the belief in a universal bond of sharing that connects all humanity." The concept of ubuntu influences the way most Africans communicate today. For instance, they are used to visitors showing up from the village without giving them prior notice or appointment. This is usually not seen as a burden or inconvenience; most Africans would rather accommodate people irrespective of the inconvenience because they believe in the universal bond of sharing that connects all humans.

Communal/Social Responsibility

From identity, the spirit of community in Africa goes on to responsibility, whereby every member of society is charged with looking out for the interests of their society as much as they look out for their own personal interests. The widely known African proverb that "A child is raised by an entire village" perfectly encapsulates this reality, and in practice it is regularly witnessed in such things as the disciplining and taking care of children – where any adult member of society has the right to mete out corrective punishment to a child they find misbehaving.

Indeed, if an individual proves to be failing in meeting their responsibility to society, the community often takes action to correct the situation. For example, if a man does not bathe and smells bad, he will be asked to take a bath. If he chooses not to, people will gang up and give him a bath to serve as an example. This is against the backdrop of a communal philosophy that one man's decision affects the other man, and that communal challenges have to be solved by the community as a whole, sometimes at the expense of individual interests.

It is very common for widows and orphans to become the full responsibility of their relatives, even distant ones. This includes, and is not limited to feeding, clothing, schooling, and all other basic needs of these individuals. This is done without any form of coercion and/or blood relationship. It is also common for relatives who are well to do to take up responsibility of other family members who aren't, ideally when a first-born gets a good job and becomes financially stable, it automatically falls to them to become responsible for their parents and siblings, including their feeding, accommodation, and schooling. This is typically done of one's free will and sense of responsibility, however the downside is an extreme increase in pressure on these individuals as they struggle to balance the rising needs of their immediate and growing family with those of their parents and siblings.

It is actually the normal practice for individuals to make sacrifices for the good of the community whenever they are in a position to do so. It is the tradition that an individual doesn't even have to be asked to surrender whatever they have that society needs, but rather they voluntarily surrender it. It is a usual practice for individuals to give up or donate their landed properties for the building and construction of schools and churches when the need arises. In the past, where the individuals didn't voluntarily surrender what they had in their possession as needed by society, the individuals would actually be forced to surrender it (in an act that was more akin to seizing). For example, if a clan wanted to provide beautiful women to the chief of a rival clan to make a peace deal, the fathers of beautiful girls would have it on their shoulders to voluntarily surrender the girls who would be found acceptable and worth the peace deal on the other side. If they refused, they would often be coerced.

Tribes, Ethnic Groups, and Clans

In Africa, ethnicity – or tribal belonging – is for many people the most important aspect of social identity after one's family. People identify more by their tribal/ethnic belongings than by their citizenship. You find someone talking about their community, and they talk of "We as Baganda," or "We as the Kikuyu," even when what they are talking about is something that they might have looked at in terms of the entire nation. For instance, in Uganda where there are about fifty-six tribes, people from a tribe will be quick to react to a new government policy as though it only affects them as a tribe. Or, if the president is from a given tribe, come the next elections, the other tribes may start to demand their turn, or come up with a candidate to represent their tribal interests, if you will, for that prestigious seat. Whereas, in the Western world, people are more attached to their citizenship and identify themselves by their nationalities. Say, the French, British, or American, and where there is an inter-country marriage, couples will even fly two flags in celebration of their identity.

There are more tribal/ethnic groupings in Africa than in any other part of the world. In simple terms, a *tribe* is a group of people who speak the same language, and it is an *ethnic grouping* when the people speak not-exactly-similar, but closely related languages so that they can fairly understand one another's language – albeit not perfectly.

Each tribe is made up of many clans, which are simply sub-divisions of people who speak the same language. This sub-division is normally according to totems, gods worshipped, differences in norms and traditions of the clan founders who go back hundreds of years.

Some tribes and ethnic groupings are spread across countries, which means that originally the people belonged to one community, but a branch migrated. Tribes and ethnic groupings are also spread across different countries because the European colonial masters who divided Africa into countries didn't endeavor to place the territory of a given tribe/ethnic group in a single country. If I went to Kenya and called on someone from the Luo tribe, they would treat me as his brother. This is because, even as a Ugandan from the Jopadhola tribe, I am well able to understand and engage in a conversation with a Luo from Kenya. And the Luo, will equally understand what I am saying, simply because legend has it that Owiny, the forefather and leader of the Kenyan Luo, was the brother of Adhola the leader of the Jopadhola found in Uganda and they separated during the Luo migration. Situations like this are common across the continent and even widespread with the Bantu-speaking group, which in collective occupies a third of the African continent.

There are many cultural differences between African tribes and ethnic groups, and this has somewhat strengthened the sense of *difference* that exists between the tribes and ethnic groups. Every tribe has its own history, customs, traditions, moral values, etiquette, and nomenclature.

For instance, when conducting marriage rituals in my tribe, the bride price is determined by the discussion of the clan elders. Whereas in another tribe, you'll find that the bride price is single-handedly determined by the girl's father. In yet another tribe, you'll find that it is determined by the girl's grandfather. Another variation is that, in one tribe, you aren't allowed to marry your close relatives such as cousins or the blood relatives of your parents, while in some tribes you are allowed to marry your cousins and even your aunts and uncles. Certain tribes do not allow marriages even someone from the same clan, much as a tracing of genealogy will reveal that the ancestor you share with that person may go back 200 or 300 years.

The tribal/ethnic differences among Africans have produced a rather deep-seated spirit of competition and segregation among the people of African nations. Tribes and ethnic groups compete for political power, for control of businesses, industries, and national resources. You find that when one tribe is in power, they largely place members of their own tribe in the key positions so as to retain power in the tribe and take a bigger share of the national *cake* into their tribe. This stirs up animosity from members of other tribes.

For social relations, in most countries, it has only been in the last two decades that people from different tribes/ethnic groups have begun to frequently intermarry. Previously, people strictly married from their own tribes/ethnic groups.

On this note of changing trends, it is important to mention that the competition and animosity between tribes and ethnic tribes have become less intense in most parts of the continent, primarily because the tribes and ethnic groups in every single country are coming to live together and closely in the urban areas, and has influenced the increasing rates of intermarriage.

It is generally a clan system – where a clan refers to relations that spread out so far and wide that sometimes one can even hardly tell how exactly they are related to the person they live with in the same house, or who they meet at a given family gathering.

Tribal segregation has been known to foster and promote nepotism, tribal conflicts, and – in many cases – civil wars. After the colonial masters formally began to exit Africa around the 1960s, many of the newly independent African nations quickly and sadly descended into a series of protracted power struggles as popular personalities, competing ethnicities, or rival regions sought to control their nation's future. Most of those power struggles unraveled into bitter inter-tribal conflicts or full-blown civil wars. Often, those wars were brutal, intense, and characterized by widespread war crimes on both sides.

In general, most of Africa's biggest conflicts can be considered to be the direct consequences of the actions by European colonial powers during the time of their selfish misrule in Africa. Many blame the divide-and-rule policies of colonial administrations for fostering mistrust, angst, and unnecessary rivalry among various ethnic groups within most countries. Others point to the fact that the colonial powers hastily withdrew from Africa, leaving power behind in the hands of ill-prepared nationalists who knew little about governance.

Aside from identity, ethnicity, and tribes is a form of expression more profound than English or other Western languages. The Mother tongue, as it is popularly called, or Mother language – which is also widely known as dialect or native language – is the indigenous language of one's parents, which is usually the first language learned by him/her. In the same vein, it is also referred to as the language of one's ethnic group. Suffice to say that, one's Mother tongue is an apparent indication of where he/she hails from.

Mother language is often regarded as one's *first language.* Therefore, by contrast, a second language is any language that one speaks other than his or her first/native language. The Mother language is noted as *first* because it is regarded as the most important language spoken by anyone due to its hereditary value as well as its cultural impact on the concerned individual.

No doubt, Mother language, or first language, contributes immensely to a child's personal, social, cultural, intellectual, educational, and economic lives. Personal, in the sense that a child's first (native) language is critical to his or her identity. Social, in the sense that when the native language of a child is not maintained, important links to family and other community members may be lost. Cultural, in the sense that sustaining a child's Mother tongue would help the child to value his or her culture and heritage, which contributes to positive self-concept.

Languages form a pivotal role in our lives as they are inclusive of our different cultures and identities. An African language is not just a series of words but, includes certain nuances that emerge in the form of idioms, metaphors, and euphemisms, as well as praises. Language is, therefore, tied intrinsically to a sense of belonging, which is in turn linked to society and its values. Research shows that these languages are frequently used by teachers to interpret knowledge from an English curriculum to African language learners.

3 - FAMILY

"A family is like a forest. When you are outside it is dense, when you are inside, you see that each tree has its place."   – Ghanan Proverb

Family Make-up and Size

Most Africa nations hold strong to patriarchal values. However, exceptions are starting to creep in. Society has undergone profound changes surrounding various aspects underlining its understanding of traditional life, in particular, family life. The concept of family is one of universal precedence amongst all Africans, whether they belong to the west, east, central, or southern regions. Family is a vital aspect of African livelihood. It is what unifies us. Like everywhere else in the world, the family is the basic unit of society in Africa. But the African family make-up is quite different from elsewhere. Whereas the nuclear family is the standard in the West, with few very close relatives, in Africa the family is in many cases a larger unit comprising of several distant relatives. In many cases, they are found living on a shared piece of land, but residing in their individual homes.

This arrangement may even include grandparents, uncles, aunts, cousins, great-grandparents, and other extended family members. It is generally a clan system – a clan refers to relations that have become so far spread out that sometimes one can even hardly tell how exactly they are related to the person. This applies even if they live within the same household or piece of land, or meet at a given family gathering.

Africans don't just live with different relatives, but actually consider those relatives as real family and relate with them in such a manner. In African culture, cousins aren't considered such, but instead, they are referred to as brothers and sisters. This is all part of how we see each other as one big family, as opposed to being separated into different households which interferes with our connection. When you grow up in this way, it makes you feel like you are a part of something larger.

Similar to other cultures, the sister to a child's father would be called their *aunt*, and the brother to a child's mother would be called their *uncle*. Yet, in an ideal African setting, a sister to their mother would also be called Mother, and a brother to their father would also be called Father. It's based on respect because they all came from one womb. Frequently, at weddings and other gatherings, an announcer might call the uncles of someone "the fathers," when really, they are the brothers of the father (uncles).

An example of this would be if I were to get in trouble with my parents, I would also have to deal with my aunts, uncles, and even grandparents. Family issues do not stay within the confines of the immediate household, but rather they are extended and dealt with by all members.

When missionaries introduced Christian faith to Africa, there was a shift in marriage practices promoting monogamy as the only biblical and morally accepted type of marriage. Monogamy, though present and practiced traditionally, was not as widely spread as polygamy.

People who chose to follow the Christian faith equated polygamy with adultery and sin, though it is still practiced within many tribes throughout the continent.

The Place of a Man

As I mentioned earlier, African societies are patrilineal, and in most cases, men are the head of the families, both nuclear as well as in the extended family. The man is the head of his household, which involves him, his wife, and their children and in some situations the man may also head a collection of different families/households. An example of this may be when a grandfather oversees leadership over different families/households.

Other men and young boys in the extended family are accorded some level of respect, depending on their age, influence, and position in the family. The process of bringing them up is designed to prepare them for the leadership of households and extended families (lineages and clans) when they mature, and this is made clear to them as early as possible. Their position as family leaders gives men specific responsibilities and roles, which they have to fulfill at all costs. These responsibilities and roles are primarily to do with providing for the family in aspects such spiritual leadership, moral guidance, food, shelter, clothing, and any other needs. It is key to note that in most African traditional settings, this division of roles and responsibilities means men aren't really involved in household chores.

As leaders, the men also have the final say on all family decisions (if it is an extended family, the men will sit and deliberate to come up with a conclusive decision). Sometimes, the men will simply dictate things. And, because of the patrilineal nature of most African societies, men (and boys who will grow into men) are also looked at as the people who hold the continuity of the family – which is sometimes referred to as a clan when talking of the extended family.

Boys are treasured more than the girls because it is they who will expand the family by producing children who, in turn, expand the family tree further and further. The girls are seen as family members who, at some point, will go away to other families of the men who will marry them, and expand those other families by giving birth.

Assuming a man is also the firstborn of his parents, he is responsible for the welfare of his siblings, parents, and his immediate family, regardless of how large it is. It's amusing to think of how much the location plays into the customs of people. Even though this information is a widespread tradition among Ugandans and other Africans alike, it is becoming more commonplace for these things to exist only in villages, since the cities have now adapted to the ways of Western culture. So, if my nieces were from the city, they would call me *Uncle*, yet if they were from the village, they would call me *Dad*.

The Place of the Woman

Male supremacy over women is vanishing to some extent. Regarding roles and responsibilities in the home, women take care of all domestic-related affairs, which are primarily household chores and nurturing their children. Women feel embarrassed if they are unable to fulfill their role as homemakers, even in situations when guests show up unexpectedly. Preparedness is a virtue imparted in the female children by their aunts that gives them control over their homes.

It's not surprising to have girls – even as early as ten-years-old – managing household duties, such as preparing meals and taking care of younger siblings. A typical village meal preparation process would require one to go and fetch water, which can be a kilometer away, then harvest vegetables. Water is required – both for the meal preparation as well as clean up. Firewood must be fetched or gathered, and then the actual food preparation and cooking can begin for whatever number of people in the given home as well as guests.

Men are not required to render assistance with domestic duties, as they are kept preoccupied with more labor-intensive duties like slaughtering cows, construction, security, and maintaining the wellbeing of the family, among other things. In many parts of Africa, concern for income-generating activities begins to create gender equality for duties.

But this does not imply that women are without respect. In fact, it is widely known that some women have more power and clout in the family than men –grandmothers are one such example.

It is vital to note that, much as the specific gender roles may seem to create a sort of imbalance, in a traditional African setting, there are no cries for equality, as it is believed that both sexes have the tasks best suited for them. There is no disrespect for either side, and dishonor only comes when these roles are challenged.

One salient misfortune is that women's inferior position in the family ascribed to them, regarding family life, is females are ineligible to inherit family property. The accepted reason is that they would get married to men from other tribes. Since each family protects their property to keep it in the family, they couldn't risk putting it in the hands of a woman who, upon marriage, would be under the authority of a man from a different tribe.

So it has always generally been considered that the woman's share lay on the side of the husband who married her who, in any case, had himself received a share from his own family – through inheritance or through being allotted a share to start and support his own family.

Parents and Children

> *The young bird does not crow until it hears the old ones.*   — Tswana proverb

Children do not question parents' authority in African culture. Rather, parents must be obeyed at all costs. And this doesn't cease to apply when one becomes an adult. From Uganda comes a proverb that perfectly captures this relationship where children will always have to listen to and respect their parents, no matter what age and social station the children have attained: "A child is always a child in the eyes of their parent." You will see for yourselves the strong influence that parents have over their children. In most ways, this is a good thing, but at times, it can be dangerous.

For example, parents will have no problem disowning their child for choosing to go against them in matters as delicate as marriage. In African societies, a great emphasis is placed upon learning to be obedient and responsible. Parents believe strongly that they need to teach their children to behave correctly. Children are taught at a very young age to do what they are told without asking for an explanation. Parents are expected to take the lead as they are viewed as more experienced and knowledgeable.

Also, unconditional respect and obedience doesn't stop at just one's biological parents but extends to all elders in one's life. For young children, discipline is meted out by any considerably older member of society. The youngest siblings are trained from childhood to respect their elder siblings. Aunts and uncles are also considered parents; they assist in the training of the children in life skills as well as in disciplining them. After all, they are quite often living in the same household and/or piece of land. Girls open up for advice or discussion to their mother or aunts more frequently, as boys do to either their father or uncles.

The young children help with housework and learn how to correctly complete household chores. The Tswana (South Africa) proverb captures this aspect of the children learning from adults how to go about household tasks: "The young bird does not crow until it hears the old ones."

In most cases, it is common for children to spend a large part of the day together, away from parental supervision. The mother is almost never the sole caregiver for the child, and from birth, the baby belongs to the whole family, frequently being looked after by siblings and older women. It is expected that older children will take an active role in both playing with the younger children and in teaching them.

From the Akan people of Ghana and Ivory Coast comes the proverb, "The old woman looks after the child to grow its teeth and the young one, in turn, looks after the old woman when she loses her teeth." The proverb perfectly points to the position of children in Africa as a parents' investment for the future. In a family with many children, the parents have hope that some will study hard and eventually liberate the family. Sacrifice means that even when a girl doesn't want to get married, she does so to help her family. Or, a boy who is now taking the position of a father and so the mother may decide to invest all the earnings they have in that boy. She will take him to school and, later, university with hope that his future earnings will save the family from poverty.

He will continue to hear Mother's, voice which says, "You are the head of the family." He gets a job, possibly marries into another culture where family, to them, is simply, "you" and "me." Yet, inside he wars with himself, knowing his family's sacrifice but he has obligations to his wife and children. Sometimes, adult men can be torn between their loyalties.

Orphans and Adopted Children

When the parents of a child/children die in Africa, in most cases, one or more of the deceased parent's siblings assumes all responsibility and becomes caretaker of the child/children. Sometimes the siblings will actually take over the running of the entire home of the deceased – in some cultures even becoming a husband to the deceased sibling's wife when it is a man who died. It is by default and not legal, although recently, it is being made legal in some countries, with the new laws based on what has always been done traditionally.

In Nigeria and many other parts of Africa, a child is regarded as social security to their parents. And so, every family desires a child. In situations where a couple faces infertility or is desirous of a male child for the continuation of the family name, every medical means, both orthodox and traditional, could be applied to remedy the situation. With recent trends of globalization and the influence of Western culture in Africa, Nigeria inclusive, child adoption is fast becoming socially and culturally acceptable. This is also supported by the fact that the cost of in-vitro fertilization and intra-gamete transfer is prohibitively expensive for many prospective adoptive parents, making the choice of adopting an infant or older child a preferable option.

When a parent is faced with circumstances that make them unable to properly raise their child, they will often give them up for adoption. However, adoption is not done legally because from the African perspective it is seen as purchasing a child, which is frowned upon. Families will raise other people's children for goodwill's sake, and not necessarily change their names to reflect the new family they are living with. Those who take in these children treat them the same as their children, and the most important element to them is the well-being of the child. If they still have relatives, occasionally they may visit to stay in contact with their ancestral roots.

Legal adoption is fast becoming commonplace in many African countries, although myths and reservations still exist, families are starting to look at formal adoption in raising a family. However, it is still fraught with many issues such as child trafficking. The buying and selling of babies have made people adhere to the traditional method of raising a relative's child.

International adoption is also on the rise among many African countries. African children have attracted attention from prospective adoptive parents from other parts of the world. Amongst other factors, there is no doubt that this recent interest is fueled by the expanded media coverage which continues to illustrate the plight of abandoned and orphaned children from Africa to audiences all over the world. This coverage emphasizes news stories that have chronicled high profile inter-country adoption cases from Africa.

Here, the inter-country adoptions by Angelina Jolie (from Ethiopia) and Madonna (from Malawi) spring to mind. Opinions are divided over the necessity and propriety of inter-country adoption. Considering the practice as a panacea for children without parents and parents without children is a prevalent view. Inter-country adoption as an opportunity to deliver children from destitute lives is a perception held by many.

However, the need to place some of the third-world children who are deprived of their family environment into homes outside of their native countries has met some resistance from the sending states, who perceive such procedures as imperialistic. Some African countries have decided to restrict inter-country adoption to certain narrowly-defined situations, and at the extreme end, there prevails a preference to prohibit inter-country adoption altogether.

Friendships and Hospitality

Friends belong to the family rather than to individuals and so are considered more or less family. African culture boasts open doors to guests at any hour of the day or night, and it is the duty of the hosts to be prepared to provide.

The necessity and role of friends to an African might perhaps be properly perceived from these two proverbs: "To be without a friend is to be poor indeed" (Tanzanian proverb), and "Friendship is a piece of dried meat, it is ever handy to save you from starvation" (Ugandan proverb).

However, care is always taken to cultivate the right friends. "Show me your friend and I will show you your character," is an African Proverb. "An intelligent enemy is better than a stupid friend," is a Senegalese proverb.

Age grades and peer groups are very common in most African societies and form the basis of many friendships. The age-grade system has long been in existence in Africa and has been recognized and used by African leaders to champion causes for the social, cultural, political, infrastructural and economic development of communities.

The interlocking responsibilities of the various grades accounted for the smooth functioning of the chief-less states. Each grade had its own social, economic and political role. The children's set covered the years of game and play. Around the ages of six and seven, however, general training and some little jobs began to be mingled with play. Primary education included story-telling, mental arithmetic, community songs and dances, learning the names of various birds and animals, the identification of poisonous snakes, local plants and trees, and how to run and climb swiftly when pursued by dangerous animals. Child training also included knowing and associating with members of one's age-group as brothers and sisters, and that they should regard them as brothers and sisters until death and even beyond.

Little chores around the house became routine, such as gathering sticks of wood for fuel, bringing water, tending the cattle, or feeding the chickens. If the child is a girl, their chores include looking after babies or younger ones, imitating mother at cooking, and trying to learn how to sew and knit. The nearest thing to the boys' political role in childhood was when he carried his father's or uncle's stool to village council meetings and listened to the interminable debates.

An age-grade usually acquires a name during its formative stage and it goes by that name until all the members are dead and the age-grade ceases to exist. Age-grades are groups of persons who, according to societal norms and values, are regarded as people of the same age. Age-grades do vary from one community to the other. In some communities, persons within a specific period of three, four, or even five years age bracket form an age-grade. In some communities, the female wing of the age-grade operates independently from the male wing. For instance, due to age differences, a man and his wife could belong to different age-grades. Also in some communities, entry into an age-grade is usually marked by an initiation rite, which may be the crowning of a long and complex preparation. In the pre-colonial period, the newly formed age-grades had to prove themselves for maturity by defending the community against hostile neighbors or enemies.

Each age-grade is given a special name that helps define its position in the community, relative to other age grades. Members of each age-grade are meant to know one another fairly well, to choose leaders among their members, to meet regularly to discuss issues of mutual or communal interest, and should be willing to help one another and defend the community when the need arises. In spite of the speed of modernization, industrialization, and urbanization, the roles of age-grades in the communities in Igbo land remain significant and impactful.

The most important roles of age-grades include unity among members, maintaining security of lives and property, enforcement of law and order, development and execution of community initiatives and projects, crime control, which is a growing area of need in many communities. Others include conflict resolution within the age-grade and in the community.

4 - LIFESTYLE

If you carry the egg basket, do not dance.
–African proverb

This is an area where many people take lightly yet a crucial factor to consider when traveling to an unknown place. If you are traveling with currency from a more developed country to a less developed country and the exchange rate may be in your favor, it is wise to plan for extra contingencies before traveling and, while there, maintain a healthy spending habit.

In Uganda and many other African countries, being largely tropical with sunshine throughout the year, there are many enticing activities going on around the city every day of the week. If you are an impulsive spender, it may be difficult to stay within budget. Safaris, hotels, and lodges around game parks will charge in US dollars even if you pay in the local currency. It will be a dollar equivalent, as these places and activities target mainly foreigners and upper-class citizens.

The minority of urban dwellers may have an advantage over villagers when it comes to transportation. In this case, there are all sorts of options ranging from flights, buses, special-hire taxis, public transport taxis, which is often a passenger van or larger buses, or motorcycle and bicycle transportation. Away from the urban areas things slow down, and not many transport companies operate in those areas. Walking or self-driving will be your main form of transport, and with this said, the locals have no sense of distance and time required for a trip as walking is part of their daily routine to get to places.

It's not surprising for someone to walk for eighty kilometers or more in a day, and when you ask how far they have to go, they will usually tell you it is not far at all. In fact, by the age of six, I was walking with my mom and siblings to and from church – which was at least sixteen kilometers away. The road was dusty and when we got closer to our destinations, we branched off to find a nearby stream or well to wash off the dust. The distance and time required that we started our journey early in the morning to make it for the only service – 9:00 am. This also happened when we went to visit our grandparents or other relatives from other villages.

Most of the Westerner countries are considered as grown economies, meaning that they have overcome the "need" level of growth and this is very evident in the infrastructural development across these nations. With this said, many African nations are still on this journey developing their infrastructure, and so you may want to consider the available transport options when you need to go to the rural areas – if you are not ready for a long, arduous journey.

It's been a blessing in disguise that people from remote parts of Africa, where they have no option but to trek long distances to get water and hunt in the wild for food, have become prominent in soccer and long-distance races and athletics.

Inclusion and Isolation

The culture is a very inclusive one, and rather than isolating one-self, people are encouraged to take part in whatever is going on.

Joining in and contributing to conversations is one of the ways people get help and solutions as opposed to holding back in fear of offending people. It's not a common thing to have personal space since that nature of livelihood does not accommodate such. The households involve everyone, and therefore, unless you are the parent in a home, you don't have the luxury of having your own room as a child or even a teenager, in some cases.

However, teenagers are encouraged to build their one or two-roomed living space on the same land as an initiation process to adulthood (this is considered a non-official house, and every tribe has a name for it). This way of life has led to tremendous liberty, even spiritually, so that emotional depression is almost unheard of. Even the elderly in communities are still actively involved in different capacities as we have seen in different chapters.

People support each other by being around. A helping hand and a listening ear is the strength of any society, and this is evident during celebrations like weddings and tragic times such as accidents and burials. People give both their time and money to be part of these events, even if they are not directly related or acquainted with the persons involved. On the other hand, Caucasian cultures commonly referred to as cold-culture climates are more stream-lined and task-oriented.

Let's take, for instance, a burial ceremony. In some African cultures, they will have a fire pit at the home of the deceased, and lots of people will gather around day and night and share in drinks, meals or conversations and memorable highlights of the deceased. This acts as a channel for positive energy and encouragement to the family of the deceased. It acknowledges the loss but gives hope and assurance for support.

In Western cultures, however, events like that are solemn and quiet. People will even dress in dark clothes and very few selected people are involved. People tend to want peace and quiet and personal space to deal with whatever has happened, and this results in isolation, depression and makes it harder to heal quicker.

Leisure and Entertainment

Africa's culture is deeply rooted in music and dance. Music has always been a channel for one's expression of both victory and loss, messages of love, sorrow and joy have all been presented through music. It's such an integral part of the African culture, with various ceremonies such as circumcision, child naming, coronation, funerals and weddings being preceded by some sort of music and dance. It's used to welcome heroes as well as portraying injustices of society.

In Kampala – the capital – and other towns within Uganda, live music has become an everyday event, and regardless of the day of the week, you'll easily find live entertainment somewhere in the city. The music style varies from one night to another.

But Africans don't just like music. They like music that they can feel. Probably you'd hear a pounding bass and catchy melodies that are memorable. Caucasians, on the other hand, are more inclined to enjoy mellow and ambient music, which is almost therapeutic.

A good example is, a couple of years ago, I was working as a sound engineer for an afro-jazz band in Kampala, and the band was playing at a multi-cultural co-operate function. A few minutes after the band started playing, a Caucasian man came to me and requested that I turn down the bass by a few decibels, which I did. Soon after he left, some Africa men came and asked whether the bass speakers were on, and expressed that they weren't feeling the groove. I was informed later that the gentleman who requested the bass to be turned down had actually hired the band to play at the event, so whatever he desired had to be met, and in this case, it was at the expense of guests who wished otherwise. People don't consider things such as going for bicycle rides and walks as leisure, as it is in most Caucasian cultures, because such activities are integrated into their daily lives and are important modes of transport.

There is a commonly known board game enjoyed across Africa. In Zambia, it is known as *cilolo*, in East Africa as *mbao*, in Ethiopia and Eritrea as *ghebeta*, and in Nigeria as *ayoo*. Music, sports and cultural dances are some kinds of entertainment that are dominant and in recent years have become a major source of income for many.

5 - HOMES AND HOME ECONOMICS

"If you pick up one end of the stick, you also pick up the other" — Ethopian proverb

The Central Homestead

In most parts of Africa, a typical home setting is in the form of a homestead. In this African context, a homestead might be described as a settlement comprised of clusters of several houses, typically occupied by a single extended family and often with attached farmland (which can be a kraal, large garden, or a hybrid of both). It is the place where members of a given family primarily live their family lives.

The homestead means that, in Africa, people construct homes around a skeleton comprising the local environment as well as the people of the community they are in (family, friends, and neighbors). Typically, the people build a house on one portion of the land and then use the other portion to grow their food and/or rear some livestock/poultry.

While this is mainly possible only in rural areas where large portions of unoccupied land exist, and people are not yet urbanized, the homestead concept still exists in urban areas. It can happen when they live on a large piece of land with their relatives and typically grow all the food that sustains them. Some will buy land and build houses not far from their relatives and then use whatever small space they can spare to grow a crop and/or to rear animals.

Houses and Housing

Traditional African architecture is, in most cases, very basic and simple, with houses constructed using barrel-modified natural materials such as poles, mud, wattle, and grass for thatching.

However, in most of Sub-Saharan Africa, the traditional basic and simple architecture only remains to be found in rural areas. In the urban areas, houses in Africa today are, in most cases, constructed after the architecture of the West, with bungalows of all sizes and designs commonly found.

The concept of renting was once alien to Africa, but over time, it has become part of the housing culture on the continent, especially in the urban areas, and has taken on its own unique African touch. Most of the rental units are made to cater to the urban poor. In most cases, the units are in the form of one or two-roomed units that are pooled together in some kind of estate.

However, over the last decade or so, modern, larger apartments have also begun to sprout up in large numbers across the continent's urban areas. These typically are a minimum of two bedrooms and are constructed in well-planned, upscale neighborhoods. Landlords most commonly demand between three months to a full year's rent, payable prior to occupancy.

Manual Execution of Household Chores - Less Machines

Appliances and gadgets that help with household chores are an alien concept in Africa. The ones that do exist are imported from the West and largely afforded by the smaller, richer percentage of the population.

Traditionally, household chores in Africa are executed manually, using only the most basic of tools. Clearing grass and other vegetation from the homestead is done with slashers, hoes, and pangas, as opposed to lawn-mowers and similar outdoor yard equipment. Sweeping the house and the compound is done with brooms, while mopping is done with rags – again as opposed to vacuum cleaners and fancy mops. Washing clothes is done by hand, in basins and buckets, in rural areas laundry happens most commonly at the village well or the riverside, as opposed to washing machines. Preparing food will normally involve lighting a charcoal stove for urban dwellers or a fireplace/campfire for those in the rural setting, and then manually doing the cooking and frying with such basic aides as mingling sticks. Ovens, coffee machines, blenders, and microwaves are a rare sight.

However, let it be mentioned that today, for those in the upper class of society, small appliances can be readily purchased locally or imported, and their use has become quite common.

Food and Diet

I have already mentioned that many Africans (especially in rural areas) live on home-grown food. One thing that is shared even by those in the cities is that Africans generally eat fresh food harvested daily from farms or gardens. While in the West, fresh food is higher priced and eaten less and choices consist more of processed food; in Africa, processed foods are hard to come by and very costly. In Africa, everyone everywhere eats fresh fruits and vegetables daily.

The environment plays a huge part in what kinds of foods are consumed in different areas of the African continent. Most cuisines include fruit, vegetables, grains, legumes, dairy, and meat products. Quite a number of cultural groups have very similar foods in their cuisines. For example, a very common maize/corn-based dish is pap, also named ugali, sadza, nsima, nchima, chima, posho, tuozafi, ubgali, bugali, sokoro, sokora, depending on which part of the continent you are eating it.

Another key thing is that Africans generally are accustomed to solid meals two or three times a day as opposed to cereals, soups, and sandwiches. They will normally have as the main course, a starch option such as sweet potato, cassava, green banana, cassava pap, or wheat pap. Then they will have a bean soup, beef stew, or groundnut paste as the gravy or sauce to accommodate along with cooked local greens.

The vital thing about foods from different cultures is having an open mind and being willing to try new things. At one time, pizza was a no-no for me. I looked at it as a mass of confusion in the name of food. It seemed like it was developed as a result of lack of groceries and so everything was used sparingly. But over time and after trying it out, it's become my go-to food for when my wife asks me if I want to make dinner. I order pizza.

When my wife first visited my family in the village, we were served millet bread/Kalo, our traditional staple food. She found it so heavy in the gut, she compared it to eating sandy play dough that wouldn't digest. Over time, she has grown to enjoy it, along with our children. We eat it fairly regularly with fish or beef stew. So as a traveler, you have to be open-minded and willing to learn the good culture of your hosts.

6 - WORK, MONEY, LAND, AND WEALTH

"You have little power over what's not yours."
— Zimbabwean proverb

Everyone Must Work

The proverb — just above — points to the fact that work is highly valued, in fact, it's a non-negotiable part of life. Everyone is expected to work and be productive in some way. As some proverbs indicate, society will look down upon and chastise the person who doesn't work, while those who work and prosper are seen as honorable and respected. Even when a person does a job which isn't so glamorous or which doesn't pay much — for instance, mending old shoes by the roadside or sweeping people's compounds — they are not looked down on. People who endeavor to be productive are respected and honored in society.

There is work for everyone in a traditional African setting, usually provided by the community. In the system of communal responsibility and accountability, the community endeavors to ensure that every person has a job and is productive. In this way, everyone is able to support themselves and their families. The wealthier men of the community who possess the means of production have additional responsibilities. The men with this ability are to provide for others who need more support. They must offer less fortunate people the opportunity to be productive and support themselves.

For example, the man who owns a lot of arable land will hire it out to those who do not own any land to grow their food, and they will, in turn, share their harvest with the landlord. One might wonder why high rates of unemployment are prevalent in African countries today. This can once again be traced to the adoption of Western culture and young people seeking more prestigious white-collar jobs. Another factor can be linked to increased selfishness and greed of any leaders of society as well as numerous wars across the continent which destabilized the ways of life of African people. This left a very young generation of uncultured youth without mentors.

While going about the process of working and being economically productive, honesty and trustworthiness are things everyone is required and expected to observe. The person who is known to be honest and trustworthy is highly esteemed and will, thus, receive many opportunities to work and earn. But the person who is dishonest and untrustworthy will be shunned by most.

Africa is a continent where the sense of community is high so, a person's reputation can hardly be kept under the rug.

Jobs (Formal Employment, Private Business)

Specialization in labor has been a part of the African lifestyle as long as recorded history has existed. There were always those whose job was to make clothes, those whose vocation was to fish, those who tended to livestock in the fields, those who raised crops on the farmlands, and so on. In that, you might say jobs and career specialization are traditionally a part of the economic system.

What is relatively new is formal employment, the formal holding of jobs in production houses and business entities owned by other people. People would most commonly apply their skills in their own ventures. Historically, every farmer grew their own crops on their own land, or herdsmen tended their own family's cattle.

Service providers would be called upon to provide their services as individuals, such as thatching a house, rather than be under a company where clients don't deal with the service providers directly. Only over the last century or so has the holding of formal jobs become a universal part of the African lifestyle. The holding of a formal job has become very prestigious, as well as a reliable assurance of a decent livelihood.

Although the African continent has been blessed with gold, diamonds, oil, coltan, bauxite, uranium, iron ore, and other valuable resources, its inhabitants have long numbered among the world's poorest. While a few sub-Saharan nations are doing relatively well, most are mired in poverty. That a continent's abundant natural resources can, in so many cases, have so little effect on its people's quality of life over so many years is one of the great mysteries surrounding the grouping of forty-nine nations located south of the Sahara Desert.

Outsiders often think of Africa as a great drain of philanthropy, a continent that guzzles aid to no avail and contributes little to the global economy in return. But look more closely at the resource industry, and the relationship between Africa and the rest of the world looks rather different.

Today, self-employment in private business is becoming the most sought-after way of making a living, However, this may not be reliable, with fast-growing economies and quickly spiraling populations. African countries are, today, considered virgin ground for many kinds of businesses. Many natives are jumping into the fray to make an income by providing much-needed goods and services alongside the Asians who, in many African countries, have long been the masters of trade and industry. Those who can find the resources to import goods from overseas (especially Asia and Europe) are making big profits as most African economies rely on importation for a certain amount of the goods that keep them going.

Wealth Accumulation, Catering for Future Generations

The Yoruba proverb, "Where you will sit when you are old shows where you stood in youth" and its Ugandan partner, "Old men sit in the shade because they planted a tree many years before," are perfect reflections of the great value attached to wealth accumulation in Africa. Everyone is expected to accumulate wealth for future use by saving and investing part of one's present earnings. The wealth is primarily accumulated to provide support for use during their later years, to provide an estate for their children and future descendants.

Perhaps to the two proverbs mentioned above, we can add a Sudanese one, "We desire to bequeath two things to our children; the first one is roots, the other one is wings." This more elaborate proverb captures the aspect of working hard, so as to have something to leave for one's children in order that they might build on it to live good lives.

Yet, even as wealth accumulation is highly valued, Africans, on the whole, recognize that money and wealth aren't the goals for all life's needs, and indeed will take effort to ensure that this reality remains in the front of their minds. The culture does not approve of acquiring wealth via dubious means, say through embezzlement or theft. Persons known to have acquired their wealth this way are generally looked down upon and not respected.

The Land Complexity

Land holds a special place regarding wealth accumulation and providing for future generations. It is the most valuable and most important resource on the continent and therefore, in many cases, a key determinant of one's economic standing.

To us, land is sacred because it is the resource around which a traditional African existence rotates. On land, one lives and survives and maybe even thrives, builds a house, grows crops, rears animals, and it provides their livelihood. In many cases, you'll find that the land in the possession of a given individual or family belonged to his/their ancestors and has been passed down through the generations. In this case, it is traditionally the role of the father to make sure there is land for all the boys he raises. The allocation is divided based on equal portions for each of the boys. Men will remain on their portion of land until they die. Sisters, who never marry and move away, will stay with their family.

Ownership, control, distribution, and access to land have historically been used to dominate and empower different nations, races, genders, and classes in Africa. Even during the pre-colonial era, land was used to create and destroy empires and nations. The Bantu migrations from the western and central parts of Africa downward, more than a thousand years ago, were, in part, necessitated by conflict over the control of agricultural, grazing, and hunting lands. The same can be said of the Mfecane period in Southern African history in the nineteenth century.

We can point out many other examples, but the important point here is that the struggle for control and ownership of land in the pre-colonial period left a political legacy of large and dominant states such as the Buganda Kingdom in Eastern Africa and the Zulu nation in Southern Africa. Alongside these dominant political entities, there are numerous small ethnic groups and small states. Relations between these ethnic groups and nations have not always been smooth. During the colonial period, contestation over land increased. The land in question became enmeshed in the race, color and ethnic divisions.

European settler economic and political systems were built on the acquisition of African land. European settler colonization in many African countries led to the expropriation of land. There are numerous examples of such struggles over land – the Shire highlands in Malawi, the Kenyan Highlands, the land question in South Africa and Zimbabwe – while the Algerian land struggle against French colonization led to one of the longest and most gruesome wars for independence.

During the colonial era, contention and conflict over land tended to assume more than just racial undercurrents. Religious institutions and the church acquired vast holdings of land and added a complex dimension to the land question. The church benefited from the colonial inequalities, and the promotion of Christianity went a long way toward the undermining of African traditional cultures and beliefs.

I propose that the colonial domination of land by the settler governments and Christian religious institutions undermined the local economic and cultural traditions, which were centered on the ownership and control of land, as well as subsequent production on the land. Some chiefs and ethnic groups which supported the dominant colonial superstructure and those that readily accepted Christianity also benefited from generous land grants during the colonial period. At that time, the majority of African peasants were forced into reserves or Bantustans. Thus, we may want to evaluate the benefits and costs of the colonial intrusions, westernization onto African soil, so that we can build on the strengths and learn from the mistakes of the past.

This ancestral land is vitally important because it is also where all family members are buried – when a person dies no matter their location, they are returned to their homeland and buried there. The land is never for sale because it is considered a memorial ground. Family or clan members, even villagers, will, in many cases, gang up and beat those who decide to individually sell this ancestral land.

Thus, land is a legacy as well as wealth in Africa. To some extent, the same is true in Canada and many other Western countries, especially if you're to look at it from the perspective of family farms and acreages.

Land was one of the pillars of the liberation movement in Africa. The post-colonial regimes have not adequately addressed the land question. There is a general failure to equitably redistribute land.

In this regard, disputes and contestation over the control of land have occurred between and within states. Inter-state contests over land resources are mainly the result of the failure of colonial boundaries to adequately address and meet the needs and goals of the African people.

In Eastern Africa, for instance, the movement of Maasai cattle herders across borders has often created border disputes between Kenya, Tanzania, and Uganda, while cementing social and economic ties within one ethnic group living in different countries.

Perhaps the majority of the post-independence land conflicts in Africa have been intra-state struggles. One of the fundamental causes has been the failure of the post-colonial regimes to redress the land inequalities and structural deformations inherited from the colonial periods. Despite the political changes, there has been more continuity than change in the racial and class nature of land ownership, distribution, and control in Africa.

Political independence without corresponding economic and social transformation has caused socio-economic and political clashes over land. Population growth and developmental needs have also exacerbated the struggle over land. The genocide in Rwanda and Burundi between the Hutus and the Tutsi can be traced to conflict over the control of political and economic resources, of which land is a central feature.

In Sudan, the control of land and economic resources is also tied to the political, religious, and ethnic conflict between the Northern Arabs, who are mainly Muslim, and the Southern Africans, who are predominantly Christian people. In many other African countries including Zimbabwe, South Africa, and Algeria, failure to redress the colonial land and economic resource maldistribution could potentially wreak havoc and has, indeed, caused some confrontation among the different racial and ethnic groups and classes of people.

Women in Production and Wealth Accumulation

Traditionally, women have recognized and hold vital roles in the economic well-being of their communities. Among the Kikuyu of Kenya, women were the major food producers. Thus, they not only had ready access to land but also had authority over how the land was to be used and cultivated. Therefore, the value of women's productive labor in producing and processing food established and maintained their rights in the domestic and other spheres. Nowadays, although women still are major food producers, either directly or through employment, they do not receive the recognition and respect that they used to. Colonialism profoundly negatively affected the role and status of women in African society. There is a section dedicated to colonialism and its impact on the status and roles of women in Africa.

African women constitute seventy-percent of the informal economy and one-third of Africa's formal small and medium-sized enterprises (SMEs) are owned by women.

Right across the continent, the spirit of entrepreneurship is evident: of all private enterprises in Ghana, forty-four-percent are led by women and on the other side of the continent in Rwanda the figure stands at forty-one-percent. While many of these enterprises might be described as small family-run affairs, it does not stop them from pointing to a female population that is keen and willing to work and pertinently, is already playing a significant role in their respective country's economies.

The challenges that are faced by African women entrepreneurs are largely no different from their male counterparts: affordable and reliable energy sources, better infrastructure, intra-continental trade agreements and improved ITC provision, the wish-list of requirements remains the same. However, African women entrepreneurs also face bigger challenges than men across the continent in starting or expanding their businesses. For example, even though over eighty-percent of the Nigerian farming workforce are women, less than five percent of landowners are women. In many countries, African women are barred from inheriting property – a key element of wealth transfer – which means women are disproportionally excluded in wealth distribution and redistribution.

Access to finance is another major issue for women entrepreneurs as financial institutions, creditors, clients, and suppliers are less willing to lend to women business owners. There is also a lack of investor confidence in women entrepreneurs on the continent where investors would invest in men rather than women. Many initiatives led by foreign development institutions were, in the past, restricted to men, but this is changing as more research shows that investments in women lead to more impact in economic development.

Moreover, in much of pre-colonial Africa, bride wealth gave women a certain amount of economic independence and clout.

In the past, African women in some societies retained a measure of control over their bride wealth which economically empowered her to a certain extent. Sadly, with the new financial constraints experienced by males due to colonialism, especially in the form of heavy taxation, bride wealth became a source of income that males sought to control. Thus, once more, women were excluded from a culture that had previously given women some measure of economic independence.

Among the Egba of Nigeria, women were the economic powerhouses of the nation due to the trade and market system they had developed. Among these people from West Africa, women dominated the trade and merchant exchange of goods of their community. Women were responsible for a number of things including: setting the rules of trade among themselves i.e., market taxes and tariffs; organizing and managing the market system; agreeing on lucrative terms of trade with outsiders; holding meetings to discuss how to improve their trade, marketing systems and more.

These women had highly developed business acumen which they used for the economic empowerment of their community. Keep in mind that many of these women were taking over the business from mothers or aunties of the same profession. Therefore, the economic knowledge they implemented had been honed for centuries. In short, they knew what they were doing.

To this day, women still dominate the local market scenes in Africa, but very few can be found in the formal Western-style economic institutions that have developed in Africa since independence. Perhaps the absence of women, and thus the absence of ancient African economic knowledge is contributing to the lack of economic organization and power in many African nations.

7 - ROMANCE, DATING, AND MARRIAGE

"If you marry a monkey for his wealth, the money goes and the monkey stays." — African proverb

The Perfect Spouse

Physical beauty is key. Like everywhere else, it is agreed that there must be a physical attraction between a couple for them to have a successful relationship. The African ideals of beauty, however, are rather different from what is considered beautiful in the rest of the world. In most parts of Africa, a lady is considered beautiful if she has a full and rounded body, in many cases, also with wide eyes. Other features of women's beauty across most of Africa include a light skin complexion, a graceful neck that is, preferably, segmented, and a gap in the front teeth, among other features.

Physical beauty is scarcely a priority when considering men in Africa, although a handsome man is largely one who is tall and thick muscled, preferably dark in most cultures but light-skinned in some.

But physical beauty is not everything. Conduct and character are of more value. The person must be hardworking (both men and women have specific roles were hard work is treasured). They must have good social manners – dress smartly, speak politely, respect elders, have a good record of not engaging in criminal and other dishonorable activities.

Background is also very key. A potential spouse who comes from a powerful family (the family of a political leader or a rich businessman) is extremely desirable to some. People coming from families that are known to engage in distasteful practices (witchcraft, cannibalism) do not normally meet with approval.

A husband was usually older than his wife and it didn't matter how much older. It was common for brides to get married to men who were as much as a decade older.

Relationships

Courting in Africa, before the influence of Western culture, was rarely an issue of a man and a woman seeing each other and then falling in love. The process was rather more the business of the entire community from which the couple came. The aunties and uncles of the girls normally identified for her the partner to marry and went about marrying her off, sometimes without even first consulting her and asking if she approved of the suitor.

Where there was prior knowledge of each other, it was normal that the man simply knew the girl but didn't really have prior rapport with her (this was the most common case). But most often, the couple would have hardly seen each other before and were brought together simply on the arrangement of their families or clans. It was unheard of in Africa for a woman to look for a man, let alone make any kind of move on a man with the intent of securing a relationship.

That background largely casts its shadow over the culture of dating/courting in Africa today, in that most times, the couple starting a relationship hardly approaches one another directly upon first sight. Rather, the man normally finds an intermediary who can approach the lady and convey his intentions. Then the two can meet and take it up from there.

However, let it also be said that today, as Western culture takes over, trends like online dating, blind dating, and even group dating are beginning to become commonplace. Women in Africa today are also chasing and going after men, even doing the actual marrying in role reversal scenarios.

Formalizing Relationships (the Wedding Process)

The formalization of relationships has always been a very important and prestigious event. The process is never an affair of the couple simply getting married. Rather, it is a large communal affair where the families and friends of the couple are central, sometimes even involving an entire clan (a collection of extended families that share a common ancestry). In most cases, family and friends may take over the organization of the function from the couple. Meetings are called where friends and family contribute funds to help make the event a success. And the bigger the functions/feasts, the more prestige and honor the couple and their families win from the community, so families and friends often go out of their way to splash big money on functions.

The marriage process begins with a visit of the groom or his representatives to the woman's side to make his intentions known. Thereafter, the groom visits the girl's family with a large entourage to be officially introduced as the person becoming their son-in-law. This second visit to the bride's family is where the groom pays dowry/bride price to the lady's family. It is at this stage, in most cases, that a big feast is organized by the girl's family, and you might refer to it as a traditional wedding, organized by the bride's family.

Thereafter, a wedding ceremony and/or feast is held on the side of the man, to celebrate the acquisition/arrival of the bride. The bride's family and friends also attend this feast. Today with the infiltration of the African lifestyle by Western culture, this is normally the stage where a church wedding function is held, and thereafter, a reception feast normally occurs at a hall or a hotel.

Some cultures, however, combine the introduction and the wedding ceremony, especially those African cultures that are etched in the Islamic religion.

Living as Marrieds

> *"A happy man marries the girl he loves, but a happier man loves the girl he marries."* – African proverb

> *"A shameless woman answers back her husband."*

> *"Beauty isn't what makes a good wife."*

In African culture, the distinct roles of husband and wife in the marriage are boldly spelled out, and everyone learns their roles, right from childhood. In every family, children are prepared for the future role of husband or wife. In the majority of African societies, the man is the head of the family. His primary responsibilities include providing for the family (all material and financial needs), protecting it (from intruders), making decisions (wherever there is a choice to be made), and representing the family in the wider community (such as at meetings). It is the pride of an African man to serve his family in this way, and he knows that he is the best person for this position. If he finds himself failing at it, not only will he feel dissatisfied, but also the community will look on and scorn him.

The wife, on the other hand, is charged with looking after the household –having everything running smoothly and keeping it in order. She executes most of the household chores, with the help of the children and maybe servants –digging in the garden, preparing food, cleaning, washing, and looking after the little children. It is her critical role to be the servant of her husband, personally serving him his food and preparing for him his bath.

However, it must be noted that today, the understanding of the husband's and wife's roles in the home have greatly changed, and Africans are beginning to individually design for themselves personal structures as benefits one's individual situation.

In my home, for example, I was raised to do domestic work because I had a single mother, and all my older sisters had married and moved away. When I was young, I knew that these were not things that the man of the house did, but I was never ashamed or resentful to help. In fact, I think it taught me from a young age to be thankful to have a house in which I was able to help. Now, as a husband and father, I am happy to be able to serve alongside my wife in this way.

When I was growing up, I never had the opportunity to learn from my dad, so it is very important to me that I teach my sons how to be well-rounded men. There is never extra time for these things, but it truly matters to make the opportunities happen because you will be the best mentor that your child will ever have.

A sad memory that I carry is the only real memory that I have of my dad. It was when I saw him at his own funeral. Everyone was gathered around him, mourning. Due to this, I think it made me become determined to have a very positive effect on my own children while I'm still here. That said, growing up, I used to hear stories about my father from village people, and how much more it would have impacted my life to be able to walk alongside him. Thus, I have learned that I have to utilize the little time that I have with my children before they are grown, and I am gone. These can be simple tasks like praying for them, helping them bathe and dress, and teaching them how to help clean around the house.

Divorce is a very infrequent thing in African culture – it is almost unheard of. As such, it seldom resonates as an option to solve a couple's marital issues. If a husband and a wife have a dispute or quarrel, they sort it out. If they can't, they go to their family elders, who normally will constitute a council of sorts to hear out the queries and help them solve the conflict. In very rare cases, a dispute is resolved by sanctioning the separation of husband and wife (when the elders have found separation the best possible solution).

Matters are almost never taken to court but are, instead, resolved on the family-to-family level. If the matter at hand is related to the separation of a marriage, the arbitrators will normally look at the interests of the children. In most cases, the father keeps children because he can provide for them – unless they are young and need the care of their mother. Sometimes, a couple agrees that for the sake of the children they will stay together. Whatever decision is made, normally it isn't done on paperwork but is more of a binding verbal agreement.

Inter-Cultural Relationships

Inter-cultural relationships between Africans and people of ethnic groups from other continents have become a common experience over the last two or so decades. Statistics show that about half of every ten unmarried Caucasians who travel to Africa from the Western world begin a relationship and either seriously date or even get married to an African. These Western travelers who begin relationships in Africa range from young men and women who come over as missionaries to mere tourists and expatriates who move to Africa in a professional capacity.

One thing to be said to single people traveling to Africa from the West is to be open to finding love. Love is an exciting journey, no matter where one finds it, and one should always be open to finding it anywhere.

However, a person from the West who finds love in Africa must be ready to face a few challenges that they might not have faced if they were in a relationship with someone from their own cultural background. Of course, the African person making the other half of the relationship will also face their own challenges.

These will primarily arise from the two people coming from different cultural backgrounds and, therefore, having different values and lifestyles in general. In this case, the couple has to purposely work on finding a common ground where they come to possess common values and lifestyle practices. One must make the effort to understand and appreciate the culture and values of the other.

As a foreigner choosing a partner from another culture altogether, you have to expect some kind of resentment from a few people in the society. It's natural, so be prepared for it and know how to appropriately handle it. There is sometimes controversy when a European man comes and wants to marry an African girl, because almost everyone feels very uncomfortable going through the process, yet it must be done.

The people always will insist on having a traditional ceremony first and then a modern one to follow.

If you are a lady marrying into an African family, when you are married, there is usually an expectation from the family that you will be giving birth within a year, so family members and other villagers will count the days. If it is taking too long, the elderly will politely reach out to you and ask if you are ill or if you are choosing not to give birth. The elders must know so that they can intervene because children are highly valued in the culture. They are seen as blessings.

8 - RACIAL RELATIONS (RACE OR GRACE?)

"No one is born hating another person because of the color of his skin, or his background, or his religion. People must learn to hate, and if they can learn to hate, they can be taught to love, for love comes more naturally to the human heart than its opposite."
— Nelson Mandela

Since the beginning of racial segregation, the topic of race and color has been – and still is – a sensitive topic. Perhaps for you reading this book, it's not of great importance, but rather something mentioned Occasionally on the newscasts and daily tabloids. And as you listen to people discuss this topic, you remain unaffected. But for people who are in cross-racial relationships, racial segregation is a concern, and they have to face it possibly on a daily basis.

As I write this section of the book, I can't help but remember a song my nieces learned in Sunday school. "Jesus loves the little children. All the children of the world, red and yellow, black and white, they are precious in His sight, Jesus loves the little children of the world." By Cendermont Kids. Source : www.cedarmont.

com. When I heard them sing it, for a moment I thought, That's a good song!

But when I started looking at the colors representing human beings, I grew disturbed. This feeling of being bothered by the song lasted for many years, leading me to start looking at people's colors with a hope that I would, one day, find a red and yellow, black and white person. I am a Ugandan, and a native African, so in this case, the color black would represent me. However, in my traveling and interacting with even the darkest Africans (and there are extremely dark Africans), I have never seen a single black person. Even when I moved to North America, I was curious to see a white person, but my search was in vain.

When I go to my ancestral home with my wife, it is a visit that should be unannounced. It will become a public affair. News will spread so fast that a Caucasian is in the area, and people will come to witness the event. They will ask me all sorts of questions, even question like "Does she talk?" or "What kind of food does she eat?" or "How do you communicate?" The questions go on and on. Meanwhile, my wife notices all these people lining up to greet her, each making sure they receive a handshake. It is possibly the only encounter they will ever have with a Caucasian in their lifetime.

In the opposite situation, an innocent Caucasian child might look at someone who is dark-skinned, like me, and think, Why doesn't he take a bath? He is all covered in dirt or grease.

No matter if it is a Caucasian person visiting a country in Africa, or an African visiting North America, people who have never met people of other races are often left with questions.

At this point, it doesn't matter who you are or what your status quo is. If you are in a cross-racial relationship, your relationship ceases to be a racial issue, because at one point you will be in the majority and among the minority at another.

By default, I like to think that racism is an issue of that heart for those whose hearts have not been transformed by the power of God in Christ Jesus.

So I will caution you here and say that, when going to Africa, one thing you should be prepared for is finding yourself physically standing out from the masses because of your skin color. You will attract (unwanted) attention to yourself. The attention that will come your way will include both good and bad, and you must be ready for it. Therefore, it is very important how you react in those situations.

Africans Esteem and Admire Western Races

The one thing that might reduce your worry and concern is that some Africans highly esteem and admire Western races, and so you won't receive much abuse, but rather attention with a tone of esteem and admiration. Where Africans who face racism in the West have to almost exclusively face negative attention and even abuse (being perceived as primitive or not beautiful); Caucasians in Africa are largely esteemed and admired.

The word Mzungu, which is used to refer to a Caucasian from most of East and Central Africa, thus has positive connotations in the eyes of the locals. If you're the type that loves being flattered and put on a pedestal as a superior person, you'll actually like the attention your skin color attracts you in Africa – only those averse to this will have a difficult time.

I know some individuals who openly admit that they enjoy being given priority because of their skin color at restaurants, supermarkets, and other public places where they'll quickly and respectfully be served. If you are a Caucasian, almost everyone will try to treat you positively and be in your good graces.

Only on rare occasions will you be subjected to real race-inspired abuse and injustice and, in most cases, this will only happen if you have personally offended a person. This is often referred to as reverse racism. "Reverse racism" is thus not racism in the real sense of the word, but it could be described as intolerance, hatred, or vengefulness based on race. If you are one of those bothered by "reverse racism," the best medicine is to fight white racism by helping to build a more just and equal society. The quicker we can achieve that, the quicker it will disappear, and the absence of racism and inequality will become starved of oxygen.

A visitor should expect to be charged exorbitantly when making a purchase. Because it is generally assumed that people from the West have so much money, almost everyone will try to make a fortune when transacting with you – the taxi people will hike their fares, the attendants in shops and markets will exaggerate the prices, those offering you services like car repair or home appliance fixing will also charge you more than the locals pay. Some people will even simply ask you to donate large sums of money to them.

Here, it is important that you make the effort to know the actual prices/charges when transacting for goods/services, and it will even be better if you always keep the company of a native to help ascertain the prices and charges.

Need for Understanding and Acceptance/Tolerance

If one dedicates an effort to exploring and understanding why and how cultures are different, one will come to understand those differences and accept/tolerate them rather than hold negative feelings towards them. One will realize that the views of neither culture are superior to the other and that no single race is at fault, as a whole, for who they are. In this spirit, we ought to be striving to reach a healthy compromise with our acceptance of one another.

For example, a person traveling to Africa might try to understand why they will be seen as superior and thereby given a lot of unwanted attention. A little research and exploration will come handy here.

By studying African and European history, I got a bigger picture of what it means to be Ugandan. I always had an idea and knew the traditions of my family, and even my village, but in studying history across the continent, you begin to realize that there are similarities among all of us.

A person who does some personal research/studying will realize that the African perspective of people from the West is shaped by history as well as the contemporary economic and political realities of the world. They will realize that the history of slavery and colonialism is primarily the reason why many Africans detest and distrust Western people, seeing them as people who are only intent on keeping them under their feet.

Need for Working to Bring a Difference

Bringing a difference entails actively taking steps to mend the fences between one race and another wherever one might come across a gulf. Things will not work themselves out, but we, as the people involved in the situation have the responsibility to take action to bring about the positive change we want to see. If, for example, your son or daughter becomes involved in a relationship in Africa and wants to get married to an African. They've found friendship, so there's no reason you should discourage or even autocratically stop them from marrying the person just because of their race.

If you meet an African who distrusts all Caucasians, in the belief that they all come to Africa to rob the land and the people, you can actively change his perspective and thereby heal his relationship with other cultures by acting in a way that proves to him beyond all possible doubt that not all visitors to Africa are there with ill intent. You can be an example that you are not in Africa for any ulterior purposes.

However, I personally believe that racial segregation can only be wiped away by the preaching of the gospel, which has the power to save and transform lives through the working of the Holy Spirit. Only then will people know and walk in the truth that, in Jesus Christ, there is neither Jew nor Gentile, but one body with different members unified in the church. Not the congregation, domination, or the religion, but the church whose head is Jesus Christ. And comprehend that we are called to a unity that understands difference. We are not called to sameness or uniformity.

9 - ETIQUETTE AND MORAL VALUES

"He who will last among strangers must discover what is acceptable and what is unacceptable to those strangers." —Tanzanian proverb

As is the case across human civilizations, African societies have moral codes that govern how they go about their everyday life, complete with established etiquettes that guide day-to-day interactions among the people. These are perfectly built within the culture and traditions of the societies. They are simply innumerable, and some of them I have already discussed at different points in the previous chapters. To close off this write-up, I have chosen to list a few pieces (of etiquette and the moral code), which I believe are most conspicuous and important to know.

Modesty and Humility

"The lion doesn't walk with its claws exposed."
— Botswana proverb

Across African societies, there is a very high value on modesty. Modesty in speech, in dress, in every aspect of contact with others.

A person who speaks and acts arrogantly or haughtily is often disapproved of and may actually be avoided by people. Whereas, someone who is always unassuming and respectful of everyone wins much favor. It is generally held that a person isn't supposed to go around telling others of their achievements or possessions or greatness among other things, but rather let the other people see those things and extol the person for them.

There are several proverbs that discourage haughtiness and arrogance across African societies, including, "While climbing up don't urinate on those you leave down because you might need them on your way back."

Greeting people as one goes along in a place is one of the most treasured acts of humility and respect for others in most African societies. And this isn't about greeting one's family members when one wakes up in the morning. The intent is to actually greet neighbors as one goes along, greet workmates at the place of work, even greet strangers, like the people you sit next to on a bus, or the cashier at a grocery store.

Societies have their own traditional dress codes dating back centuries, and against these, every society has developed some kind of standard (or at least acceptable) dress code. And in these codes, modesty is still largely involved. The clothes are, in most cases, designed so the wearers do not reveal body parts which in many African societies are taboo to be exposed in public, such as breasts and thighs for women, and chests for men. This is a form of purity.

Honesty and Trustworthiness

"Trustworthiness makes rich." – Swahili proverb.

Being honest and trustworthy in one's dealing with others is one of the most valued and encouraged virtues across the African continent. From an early age, parents teach and encourage their children to be honest and trustworthy in all things, in all situations when dealing with others. Those who show themselves to be honest and trustworthy indeed are promoted and given responsibility ahead of those who do otherwise. More so regarding matters of business and possessions, one is expected to be honest and trustworthy, or they will lose out on so many opportunities.

These moral values include being honest and trustworthy with one's words, rather than lying and making empty promises. I learned of a story about a missionary in Zambia who lost all the beneficiaries God had sent her to serve because, unknown to her, the rural people she was working among very much judged one on their ability to fulfill promises on time or not. She had promised to build some concrete buildings to replace the wooden ones where the mission started its operations in three months. She, however, did not discuss details of fundraising, process steps, and such logistics. When there were delays in the raising of the money and three months had passed without the lady starting to construct the buildings, the people she worked with began to doubt her. They began to leave her, one after the other until, in two months, she was left with just three out of four volunteer helpers, and the people who she was working among were no longer coming to her mission for prayers and literacy lessons. What she hadn't found out was that the rural people of Africa, in most cases, judge a person by how much that person's promises come to pass.

Self-Control

"Anger and madness are brothers." – African proverb

Self-control is another thing that permeates Africa etiquette and general life ethics. Controlling one's anger, one's tongue, one's excitement, one's libido, among other things, is very treasured, and also inculcated into people when they are still children living under their parents.

For that matter, in many cultures, a person is expected not to laugh so loudly and freely when amused, but to do so in a very controlled manner. In times of anger, one is expected to control themselves and think before taking any action.

It is a matter of fact that people known to lack self-control are avoided in African society. They might even be insultingly be nicknamed according to what normally makes them act without controlling themselves. For example, if one is known to laugh out loud at anything, they can give them a nickname that indicates someone whose laughter habits have made them appear a fool. And people will also often avoid you when you can't control yourself because it is taken for a lack of decorum.

Making Peace Preferred to War (Conflict Resolution)

"In the moment of crisis, the wise build bridges and the foolish build dams."   – Nigerian proverb

Contrary to what many people outside the continent think (mostly because of the news of war and conflict that they rarely see), solving problems amicably truly matters in Africa. African culture is primarily based on openness, community, and family. When there is an issue, it normally becomes everyone's priority to fix it. If it is in the village, all people who can, will try and contribute to the peaceful resolution of the conflict.

The same when it is an inter-family, inter-clan, inter-village, inter-tribe, or international conflict. Where the conflict involves many people (say it is inter-tribe or international) meetings will be held where deliberations aimed at achieving peace will be made. These will be attended by delegates comprising leaders from the conflicting parties.

Communication is Vital, and Always Measured

Communication in Africa is also very highly valued, however, it is also important to note that in Africa this differs in some very significant ways from what it is like in the West. When you communicate in Africa, you consider the feelings of society. Like many other facets of African culture/lifestyle, communication is modeled after decades or centuries ago.

In verbal communication, subtlety is often very treasured. At least if one is to be considered civilized and a person of decorum, one has to mind not to offend others in their speech. For this reason, there are a lot of euphemisms, proverbs, and other tools that help deliver messages in a subtle or even indirect way. People very often imply things rather than state them clearly.

For example, there was a beautiful girl who went to church and forgot to brush her teeth. When her aunt realized this, she didn't confront her, she bought chewing gum and started chewing some and offered some to her daughter/niece, the girl then realized her mistake. Or, if a couple is having an argument, and the lady is not getting results, she will go and talk to her husband's best friend, so that when the best friend talks to the husband, he has information and will communicate in such a way that the husband will realize that he has not been treating his wife well.

Aesthetics and beauty, or artistry, are also highly valued and a big part of African communication. So, if you're new to Africa, you might find many people speaking in a way that might seem redundant and unnecessarily winding, but if you look closer you will find that it is all intended to inject some artistry or aesthetics into the delivery of the message. Proverbs, idioms, jargon, wise sayings, and the like are thus a key part of African day-to-day communication –at home, at work, in the street, and at functions.

The language barrier between North Americans and Africans is often not necessarily a translation issue or an accent issue, where the Africans communicating speak a Western language. It is simply that the Africans aren't very direct with their words. Another reason for African communication not being very direct is that in many cases Africans use codes for certain purposes.

Say when talking in the presence of children and they don't want the children to understand things that are for adults – they can talk of lovers' bedroom time as merely *holding a conversation*.

But on the whole, Africans are people who believe in communication and always endeavor to have meaningful relationships.

Sharing and Kindness

These two positive characteristics simply have to be the key to the African lifestyle, since African society is built around – and for – the community as a whole. As such, Africans don't simply stop at having a communal identity, working together, or mourning together in difficult times. Rather, they also share both material and non-material things.

You might be shocked to see a neighbor who has run out of salt or sugar come to ask for some from you, either because they can't afford to buy more at the moment or because the shops are far from home to walk there. But this is normal for those who live by traditional African values. Since time immemorial, Africans and their neighbors have always shared things, everyone seeking what they are lacking from the people around. In the rural areas, people will come and pick a few burning coals from your stove in order to help them light their own stove. After harvest, families will send something to the neighbors, relatives, and friends.

It is also all part of the expectation of kindness that African society places on every member. If you are still youthful, you are not expected to be walking on the road and pass an old man struggling with a heavy load, you're expected to offer the man some help. No one is expected to also freely give physical things; sharing belongings is widely practiced. If you have something, you are to give it to another person if needed. We are, after all, a community, and the way to succeed as such is by working together. A few other precepts include;

- Respect for elders (*He who doesn't fear elders meets an early death* –Ugandan proverb),

- Searching for and applying wisdom (*Wisdom is like fire: people take it from others* – Congolese proverb)

Guarding the inside secrets of one's community (Home affairs are not talked about in the public square –Nigerian proverb) are among other pieces of African etiquette that are very highly valued.

10 - FINDING NORMAL

"No matter how many times you wash a goat, it will still smell like a goat." — Ethiopian proverb

When you are set to leave for a journey, everything is well prepared. Even your mind is already set to the fact you are leaving for somewhere else. You have your bags packed and the necessary documents with you. All that remains is to get going on your journey.

Ordinarily, you are seen off at the airport if taking a flight or to the bus station or train station, depending on the means of travel you choose. You are either seen off by your relatives, best friends or even family members and they are the ones who ensure you get there on time. Then, of course, there is the need to be seen off by close ones. A good send-off gives one memory to hold on to, of where they've been.

Before you depart, they kiss you goodbye, and with the hope of seeing each other again soon enough, you are set for your trip. With a final glance around, you head to the means of transport for the journey. Memories of where you come from assail you, making you depart with a heavy heart. Those emotions are made worse by the fact that you are going to an altogether new place.

There's no telling what lies ahead of you, and it's normal to feel anxious. Hopefully, you'll soon be back to the familiar place.

Soon you are on your way, and while on the flight or whatever other transportation you use, look at what nature has to offer through the windows or perhaps flip through a magazine. You have a lot of time ahead of you on anyway during the entire journey, so it is best if you keep yourself occupied.

Every so often, thoughts of people you've left behind come to mind and you push it away by staring outside. There's really no reason to be anxious about what lies ahead, after all you've done enough research from available resources. You may even have a book about the people and places you are heading to and start to read it to occupy your mind. This is all done in a bid to fit in easily when you get there.

Perhaps you even decide to take a nap to pass the time. That comes easily, considering you had a late night the previous day. Eventually, you doze off, only to awaken on arrival to your destination. With one glance, you take in as much as you can of your new surroundings. It is not quite what you thought it would be, but you take a step towards what lies ahead.

Your host is waiting to give you a royal welcome. Happy to have someone waiting to receive you, you let out a sigh of relief on seeing him. You've heard stories of people being stranded in new places and hoped it would not happen to you. Thankfully he's here, and you walk towards each other and are soon engulfed in a warm hug. With another look, you take in the new place as a new experience starts to unfold. It will possibly change your frame of thought from that time on even though you may not know it yet. You are confident as you take on what lies ahead of you with support of your host.

It's one thing to talk to a soldier who's joined the military because of passion, love, and patriotism, but it's another thing to talk to a soldier whose only hope in protecting his family was to join the military at the age of seventeen. The later conversation is filled with details of despair that led him to take that step.

This story reaches home with me, in that my elder brother was caught up in something like this. He was in the middle of the war between the rebel forces and the ruling government of Uganda, back in the early eighties. Probably at the age of fifteen, he joined the army to save his life. I'd not imagined anything such as this so close home, and hearing him tell the story shook me more than I would have expected. He came face to face with our uncle, who also was a military man – but on the other side. The two pointed their guns at each other, but thankfully for family's sake, their story ended well as none of them was hurt. For the south Sudanese soldier who was forty-years-old, at the time of our conversation, I learned that he'd already been involved in numerous battles and had already been shot five times. He showed me the bullet scars and explained in detail the battles where each was sustained. It surprised me how much detail he'd remembered about how each scar came about. I kept wondering whether he was not tired of all the battles he'd had to fight but keenly listened to what he had to say. He was in no hurry, but recounted all the stories to me in detail, one by one. Each time he spoke, I noticed hidden pain in his words. At the time, the reason for the pain was not clear to me.

After taking in all that he had to say, I posed a question to him. "Aren't you tired of being in endless battles that are a risk to your life?" He smiled at me, then said, "Brother, when I fought to protect my people and country I did it all in ignorance not knowing what would ever happen to my body when I die. Now that I am a follower of Jesus Christ, I know my destiny." He went on to quote a scripture after that.

> Romans 14:8
> *"For if we live, we live to the Lord; and if we die, we die to the Lord. Therefore, whether we live or die, we are the Lord's."*

After a short pause, he continued. "Many of my fellow soldiers in the battlefront don't know that, and someone needs to be able to share that with them while they are out in the battlefield. There's a lot of despair and hopelessness in the field of battle. Unless they have someone to tell them of the hope we have in Christ they will otherwise lead empty lives. There is a need to tell them there is life after death in the Lord Jesus. I feel well placed to do so, since I am familiar with what goes on with them." He smiled delightfully.

I noticed the calm look that spread across his face as he said those words. He must have found peace in the midst of all that had been going on around him. That peace had emanated from the knowledge of Christ, and that he had given his life to the Lord. I am more convinced than ever before that God can be found in any situation. Like a battlefield, for example.

At that time, South Sudan was still going through the transition process and, so on the tour around, we were escorted by military men everywhere we needed to go. This made us feel important, being escorted around, we had the opportunity to interact with these men whose lives had been transformed by the power of the gospel, who had been through the chaplain program and were actively serving in the battlefield as combatants, while also attending to the spiritual needs of their troops. It was clear to me they had been through adequate training.

Quite a noble task it is, spreading hope in the midst of the chaos of war. I listened to the stories of a number of them, all culminating into how they encountered God, causing them to turn their lives around forever. That was quite an adventure and life-changing experience for me, and I had to go back to Kampala after the two weeks of location scouting for a movie about the life of chaplains that I was going to take part in.

The same may be true for you that after days, weeks months or even years of venturing in the mission field or any other episode of your life you decide it is time to leave. Maybe you are forced by circumstances to journey back, but this time it's different because you're heading back home to a community or job or a people once known to you. There's not much adjustment on your part since you are already familiar with their ways. The only things you will have to catch up with are any changes that have taken place since you left.

These few pointers will help you settle back into the place you left behind.

Ways to Find Normal.

1. Don't leave on a bad note (go with the blessings of your colleagues, friends, and family or church). It is possible

you will return, therefore do not burn bridges when you leave. If possible, make sure you are at peace with all whom you leave behind. Even if you don't return, it is good for you to leave good memories behind.

2. Keep in contact. One way for you to stay in the know is by keeping in contact. It shows that you care when you make an effort to find out how people are getting on after you leave. A simple phone call now and then or even a message sent will keep things running with you and them.

3. Expect change when you return. Nothing is permanent in life except change, and it is imminent. "The thing we oppose the most in life is change which isn't in our terms." Things are never the same as you left them, so it is best to be prepared for it.

For instance;

– The child you used to babysit ten years ago, will no longer need babysitting because he or she is now a teenager. When you meet them you will no longer bounce them on your knee as you did before. Embrace the fact that you will have to relate on a different level with them now.

– Your workplace will have new employees and even management changes. There is no assurance of seeing familiar faces or having the same routine. Things change, people leave work, and others get employed. It will be good if you expect this.

–Your church family will grow and there will be new members. No longer can you find a seat at your favorite corner as you'll find it taken already. It will certainly be different and you will have to contend with starting all over again. An American man put it this way, "What you are facing now is called reverse culture shock." Things have changed and you weren't here to change with them. This happened on my recent visit to Uganda after living in Canada for four years. I must say everything was different and there was nothing wrong with me.

–Your friends will have new friends and some of them will be married and you can't see them. People change, and things may not be the same with them anymore. This is part of the change, therefore, get ready to make new friends as well as adjust to changes with the old ones. Do not expect to relate with them the same way that you used to before you left.

–Infrastructure in your towns will change. There may be new growth, government, or policies. You will no doubt find a change in places you were previously familiar with.

4. Ask–don't be ashamed of asking questions to family members about your town. Whereas you may think that this is all common sense, you will be surprised how uncommon this sense is in this day and age where there are so many life's distractions that occupy people's minds. Go ahead, ask around, so you get to know what's been happening around.

Here's an example of how rigid people are to change. This will open your eyes so you don't get caught up in similar circumstances.

One time we were doing some floor replacement at the entrance of a gym. The time had come for a facelift and this was where we began. Knowing that this is a busy place we took safety precautions as required and blocked off the entrance. We pinned a big notice to the door that read "Door closed–Follow the arrows to enter the gym."

We also put caution tape around that entrance and leading to the alternate route to enter the gym. It was surprising, therefore, how many people came and read the notice, walked under the caution taped barricades, straight to the door, and tried to forcefully open it. They seemed completely oblivious of the fact that they were stepping on wet cement in the process. All that these people wanted was to access the gym the same way they had before.

To prove how rigid people are about change is that other people came close to the gym entrance, read the notice then turned back with frustration and murmuring. None of them were ready for the small change of taking another door.

We told the site superintendent that our work was being interrupted by people trespassing and stepping on wet floors. The superintendent looked at my colleague, who was our foreman, and said, "It's surprising how many oblivious people are out there and the more surprising thing is, how many of those people are out there who don't even know that they are in oblivion." How right he was!

But let's face it – this is not just talking about insensibility or lack of focus but the fact that sometimes we zone out and we don't get it. We have no clue why we just can't seem to get it. It's as if we are stuck at some point and we can't get ourselves around the fact things can be different, they can change. It might be that our minds get preoccupied with many things and so are unaware of our surroundings, even when we venture through it on a daily basis.

Such is the reality of life anyway and people resist change all the time. It is as if having found a sweet spot, we won't let go but hang onto it with a tight grip. Much like, we are afraid to try out the new and would rather stick to the familiar. In the same way perhaps if we get on with life with the sense of awareness that things will never be the same as we left them, resettlement in the community will be a much lighter burden to carry.

COMMONLY ASKED QUESTIONS ABOUT VISITING AFRICA

Is it safe to go to Africa?

The answer to this question is simple and straightforward! Yes, it safe to visit Africa. The only warnings to keep in mind is to stay away from areas of conflict. Aside from this, Africa is an entirely safe place.

Do people speak English in Africa?

Some of the most populated countries in Africa are English-speaking countries. Nigeria, Kenya, and South Africa are but a few of the countries in Africa with a significant percentage of the population being English speakers.

Do all Africans live in mud huts and grass-thatched houses?

No, they all don't. You may be surprised to discover that Africa has beautiful cities and well-paved roads. Some Africans beautiful have houses that will give some places in Europe and America a run for their money. However, most rural areas still live in mud and grass-thatched homes.

Can I pet an animal on a safari?

Safaris have tour guides and they have good knowledge of the animals and the right time to get close to them. However, touching a wild animal might not be advisable.

Is Africa a country?

No, it is not. This is probably the most misunderstood part of the African continent. Africa is made up of fifty-four countries and thousands of ethnic groups that are scattered across different geographic regions.

Do Africans live side by side with wild animals?

Africa is well known for its population of wild animals, but with rapid urbanization in almost all countries of the continent, the wild animals are being restricted to forest reserves and national parks that are controlled by the government.

Most wild animals are only be seen in parks and forest reserves, far away from cities and towns.

Can I get malaria when I visit?

Yes, you could. Malaria can be compared to having a bad flu and is caused by a parasite that commonly infects a certain type of mosquito that feeds on humans. You can look into preventative measures by consulting your natural/medical health practitioner before you travel. Ensuring you sleep under a mosquito net will also be helpful.

Is there electricity and running water in Africa?

Africa has cities that are similar to those that can be found in the best countries in the world. Many African countries have stable electricity and running water in their cities. This may not be the case in remote villages.

Do I need a visa to visit Africa?

Yes, you do. Like mentioned earlier, Africa is made up of fifty-four countries. As such, if you are visiting Africa, you need to know the country you plan to visit and look into getting the appropriate visa for that country.

FINAL THOUGHTS

My sincere hope is that this book will be of great help to you on your exciting adventure into Africa, regardless of the length of your stay. The things you will see will undoubtedly surprise you, and there may be times when the culture shock is all too real to deal with. While the majority of this little book has been telling you of what is different between here and there, even if you don't remember anything else, let the take-away message be to treat others as you would want to be treated, no matter what the situation may be. You will be faced with challenges, possibly even moral conflicts, but remember that if nothing else, despite coming from different lands, we are all humans and thrive on love.

CPSIA information can be obtained
at www.ICGtesting.com
Printed in the USA
BVHW052311300922
648391BV00003B/596

9 781630 505585